C000103011

Sharks

*Everything You Need to Know and More
about Sharks*

Copyright © 2020

All rights reserved.

DEDICATION

Contents

What is Sharks? 1

A Brief History of Sharks 3

Description and Habits.. 15

Some of the 400+ Species of Sharks 22

The 10 Largest Sharks 34

Sharks Facts That May Surprise You.......................................42

What is Sharks?

Most people probably think of a shark as a swimming animal with big fins and pointy teeth. But how exactly does it fit into the Animal Kingdom? For starters, some of you may be surprised to know that sharks are indeed fish. But they really don't look all that similar to your average gold fish, do they?

There's a good reason for these distinct appearances: while they are both fish, the creatures shown above actually represent two very different "Classes" of animals.

What we think of as the typical fish – goldfish, minnows, salmon – are "bony fish" belonging to Class Osteichthyes. They have a skeleton that is made mostly of bone. In addition, they are agile swimmers that can move forward and backward, and they are found in rivers, lakes and seas.

1

How Are Sharks Different From Other Types Of Fish?

Sharks, on the other hand, belong to an entirely different group called Class Chondrichthyes (which oddly enough are thought to have evolved from an earlier group of bony fish). Some newer classification schemes instead refer to this as Class Elasmobranchii. Mostly these are marine fish, meaning that they live in salt water. "Cartilaginous" fish or "elasmobranchs" include sharks along with rays, skates, and chimaeras (ratfish): those that lack true bone. Instead, they have a skeleton made of cartilage, reinforced with calcification (calcium builds up in the tissue, causing it to harden). Sharks can only swim forward. This is because unlike in bony fish, their pectoral fins can't bend upwards. Many sharks have to keep swimming in order to breathe.

Among other key distinctions, cartilaginous fish have a unique type of tooth attachment and replacement. Teeth are arranged in many rows that are constantly shed and replaced. Unlike bony fish, whose males and females eject their sperm and eggs into the water to mix, these fish have internal fertilization. "Chondrichthyan" males have organs known as claspers. These are a modified part of the pelvic fins that are inserted into the female cloaca (an opening in the body), so that sperm can be placed inside the females during copulation. Compared to bony fish, Chondrichthyans mature sexually at much greater ages, produce fewer young at a time, and can have very long gestation periods.

A Brief History of Sharks

Sharks have been around for hundreds of millions of years, appearing in the fossil record before trees even existed. But what did they evolve from, are they 'living fossils', and how did they survive five mass extinctions?

Sharks belong to a group of creatures known as cartilaginous fishes, because most of their skeleton is made from cartilage rather than bone. The only part of their skeleton not made from this soft, flexible tissue is their teeth.

The group includes the more famous animals such as whale sharks and great whites, but also all rays, skates and the little-known chimaeras (also known as ratfish, rabbit fish or ghost sharks).

While often referred to as living fossils, sharks have evolved many different guises over the hundreds of millions of years that they have been swimming the oceans.

When did sharks first appear?

The earliest fossil evidence for sharks or their ancestors are a few scales dating to 450 million years ago, during the Late Ordovician Period.

Shark-like scales from the Late Ordovician have been found, but no teeth. If these were from sharks it would suggest that the earliest forms could have been toothless. Scientists are still debating if these were true sharks or shark-like animals.

Chimaeras are cartilaginous fishes, but not technically sharks. It is thought that sharks and chimaeras may have diverged up to 420 million years ago. Today, many chimaera species are limited to the deep ocean.

Analysis of living sharks, rays and chimaeras suggests that by around 420 million years ago, the chimaeras had already split from the rest of the group. As there are no fossils of these animals from this period of time, this is based solely on the DNA and molecular evidence of modern sharks and chimaeras. It was also around this time that the first plants invaded the land.

Oldest shark teeth

The earliest shark-like teeth we have come from an Early Devonian (410-million-year-old) fossil belonging to an ancient fish called Doliodus problematicus. Described as the 'least shark-like shark', it is thought to have risen from within a group of fish known as acanthodians or spiny sharks.

Analysis of living sharks, rays and chimaeras suggests that by around 420 million years ago, the chimaeras had already split from the rest of the group. As there are no fossils of these animals from this period of time, this is based solely on the DNA and molecular evidence of modern sharks and chimaeras. It was also around this time that the first plants invaded the land.

The first recognisable sharks

By the middle of the Devonian (380 million years ago), the genus Antarctilamna had appeared, looking more like eels than sharks. It is about this time that Cladoselache also evolved. This is the first group that we would recognise as sharks today, but it may well have been part of the chimaera branch, and so technically not a shark. As active predators they had torpedo-shaped bodies, forked tails and dorsal fins.

Golden age of sharks

The Carboniferous Period (which began 359 million years ago) is known as the 'golden age of sharks'. An extinction event at the end of the Devonian killed off at least 75% of all species on Earth, including many lineages of fish that once swam the oceans. This allowed sharks to dominate, giving rise to a whole variety of shapes and forms.

Some of the most bizarre prehistoric 'sharks' to appear during this time actually evolved out of the chimaera lineage. These include Stethacanthus, which had a truly peculiar anvil-shaped fin on its back, Helicoprion with a spiral buzz saw-like bottom jaw, and Falcatus, in which the males had a long spine jutting out of the back and over the top of the head.

6

Modern-day chimaeras are much less diverse and typically live in the deep ocean. Growing up to 1.5 metres long, they are not actually sharks. Their upper jaw is fused with the skull, and most chimaera also have venomous spines.

The origin of sharks' fearsome jaws

The end of the Permian Period (252 million years ago) saw yet another mass extinction event, wiping out around 96% of all marine life. But a handful of shark lineages persisted.

By the Early Jurassic Period (195 million years ago) the oldest-known group of modern sharks, the Hexanchiformes or sixgill sharks, had evolved. They were followed during the rest of the Jurassic by most modern shark groups.

It was at this point that they evolved flexible, protruding jaws, allowing the animals to eat prey bigger than themselves, while also evolving the ability to swim faster.

Shrinking sharks

At the beginning Cretaceous of Period (145 million to 66 million years ago) sharks were once again widely common and varied in the ancient seas, before experiencing their fifth mass extinction event.

While much of life became extinct during the End-Cretaceous extinction event, including all non-avian dinosaurs, sharks once again persisted.

But they were still affected. Fossil teeth show that the asteroid strike at the end of the Cretaceous killed off many of the largest species of shark. Only the smallest and deep-water species that fed primarily on fish survived.

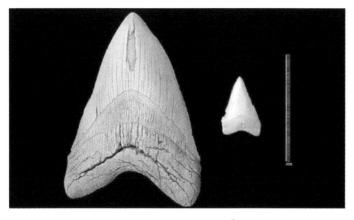

Great white shark evolution

Sharks soon began to increase in size once again, and continued to evolve larger forms throughout the Palaeogene (66 to 23 million years ago). It was during this time that Otodus obliquus, the ancestor to megalodon (Otodus megalodon), appeared.

O. megalodon is the biggest shark ever to have lived, and scientists consider it one of the most powerful predators to have evolved.

Despite what many might think, megalodon is not related to great white sharks. In fact it may have been in competition with the great white shark's ancestors, which evolved during the Middle Eocene (45 million years ago) from broad-toothed mako sharks.

Hammerhead shark evolution

The youngest living group of sharks are thought to be the distinctive hammerhead sharks.

There are at least eight different species of hammerhead shark, and while fossil teeth evidence suggests that their ancestors may have existed 45 million years ago, molecular data points to a much more recent appearance during the Neogene (which began 23 million years ago).

The strange shape of their head is thought to mainly help in electroreception (the detection of naturally occurring electric fields or currents) as they hunt for prey. It may also improve their vision, enhance their swimming and refine their ability to smell.

Since the End-Cretaceous mass extinction, sharks have come to dominate the oceans once again, returning to the role of apex predator along with large marine mammals.

Why are fossil shark teeth so common?

The vast majority of shark fossils found are teeth. This is down to two main reasons.

Because most of the skeleton of sharks is made from soft cartilage, it takes special conditions for this to preserve. The teeth, however, are made from a much tougher material known as dentin, which is harder and denser even than bone. While this enables a powerful bite, it also increases the chance that the teeth will fossilise as they are less likely to decompose.

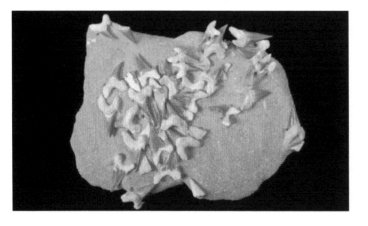

The other reason is simply numbers. Rather than having just a few sets of teeth that last all their life, sharks are continually producing new teeth. As an older one breaks or wears down, it simply falls out of the front of the mouth and onto the sea floor, as a new tooth takes its place.

Depending on species and diet, over its entire lifetime a shark can produce between 20,000 and 40,000 teeth.

This means that there is a much greater chance that a shark tooth will be preserved and turned into a fossil. Not only are the teeth the most common part of sharks to be found, they're one of the most common fossils of any organism.

How did sharks survive five mass extinction events?

There is no single reason sharks survived all five major extinction events - all had different causes and different groups of sharks pulled through each one.

One general theme, however, seems to be the survival of deep-water species and the dietary generalist. It is possible that shark diversity may also have played an important role.

Sharks are able to exploit different parts of the water column - from deep, dark oceans to shallow seas, and even river systems. They eat a wide variety of food, such as plankton, fish, crabs, seals and whales. This diversity means that sharks as a group are more likely to survive if things in the oceans change.

Rather than sharks simply being incredibly hardy, it is more likely that their amazing diversity is the key to their success. It's no wonder they've been dominating the ocean for hundreds of millions of years.

Sharks Today

Today, sharks and humans have a complicated relationship. Shark populations are in severe decline due to human activities, and without immediate action, scientists are predicting that sharks could be facing extinction for the first time in history. However, shark ecotourism has allowed nations to offer protection to sharks, and as research into sharks increases, scientists are hoping to discover new ways to protect them.

Description and Habits

There are several hundred species of sharks, ranging in size from less than eight inches to over 65 feet, and native to every marine environment around the world. These amazing animals have a fierce reputation and fascinating biology.

Fast Facts: Sharks

- Scientific Name: Elasmobranchii
- Common Name: Sharks
- Basic Animal Group: Fish
- Size: 8 inches to 65 feet
- Weight: Up to 11 tons

- Lifespan: 20–150 years

- Diet: Carnivore

- Habitat: Marine, coastal and oceanic habitats worldwide

- Conservation Status: 32% are Threatened, with 6% as Endangered and 26% as Vulnerable on a global basis; 24% are Near Threatened

Description

A cartilaginous fish has a body structure formed of cartilage, instead of bone. Unlike the fins of bony fishes, the fins of cartilaginous fish cannot change shape or fold alongside their body. Even though sharks don't have a bony skeleton like many other fish, they are still categorized with other vertebrates in the Phylum Chordata, Subphylum Vertebrata, and Class Elasmobranchii. This class is made up of about 1,000 species of sharks, skates, and rays.

Sharks' teeth don't have roots, so they usually fall out after about a week. However, sharks have replacements arranged in rows and a new one can move in within one day to take the old one's place. Sharks have between five and 15 rows of teeth in each jaw, with most having five rows. A shark has tough skin that is covered by dermal denticles, which are small plates covered with enamel, similar to that found on our teeth.

Species

Sharks come in a wide variety of shapes, sizes and even colors. The largest shark and the largest fish in the world is the whale shark (Rhincodon typus), which is believed to reach a maximum length of 65 feet. The smallest shark is thought to be the dwarf lantern shark (Etmopterus perryi), a rare deep-sea species which is about 6 to 8 inches long.

Habitat and Range

Sharks are found from shallow to deep sea environments, in coastal, marine and oceanic environments the world over. Some species inhabit shallow, coastal regions, while others live in deep waters, on the ocean floor and in the open ocean. A few species, such as the bull shark, move easily through salt, fresh and brackish waters.

Diet and Behavior

Sharks are carnivores, and they primarily hunt and eat fish, sea mammals like dolphins and seals, and other sharks. Some species prefer or include turtles and seagulls, crustaceans and mollusks, and plankton and krill in their diets.

Sharks have a lateral line system along their sides which detects water movements. This helps the shark find prey and navigate around other objects at night or when water visibility is poor. The lateral line system is made up of a network of fluid-filled canals beneath the shark's skin. Pressure waves in the ocean water around the shark vibrate this liquid. This, in turn, is transmitted to jelly in the system, which transmits to the shark's nerve endings and the message is relayed to the brain.

Sharks need to keep water moving over their gills to receive necessary oxygen. Not all sharks need to move constantly, though. Some sharks have spiracles, a small opening behind their eyes, that force water across the shark's gills so the shark can be still when it rests.

Sharks that do need to swim constantly have active and restful periods rather than undergoing deep sleep like we do. They seem to be "sleep swimming," with parts of their brain appearing less active while they remain swimming.

Reproduction and Offspring

Some shark species are oviparous, meaning they lay eggs. Others are viviparous and give birth to live young. Within these live-bearing species, some have a placenta just like human babies do, and others do not. In those cases, the shark embryos get their nutrition from a yolk sac or unfertilized egg capsules filled with yolk.

With the sand tiger shark, things are pretty competitive. The two largest embryos consume the other embryos of the litter.

While nobody seems to know for certain, it has been estimated that the whale shark, the largest shark species, can live up to 150 years, and many of the smaller sharks can live between 20 and 30 years.

Sharks and Humans

Bad publicity around a few shark species has doomed sharks in general to the misconception that they are vicious man-eaters. In fact, only 10 out of all the shark species are considered dangerous to humans. All sharks should be treated with respect, though, as they are predators, often with sharp teeth that could inflict wounds (especially if the shark is provoked or feels threatened).

Threats

Humans are a greater threat to sharks than sharks are to us. Many shark species are threatened by fishing or bycatch, which lead to the deaths of millions of sharks each year. Compare that to shark attack statistics——while a shark attack is a horrifying thing, there are only about 10 fatalities worldwide each year due to sharks.

Since they are long-lived species and only have a few young at once, sharks are vulnerable to overfishing. Many are caught incidentally in fisheries targeting tunas and billfishes, and a growing market for shark fins and meat for restaurants is also impacting different species. One threat is the wasteful practice of shark-finning, a cruel practice in which the shark's fins are cut off while the rest of the shark is thrown back in the sea.

Some of the 400+ Species of Sharks

All organisms have scientific names, a name that is unique for each species. Every species has two Latin names which allow people to be certain they are talking about the same creature no matter what language they speak.

For example, the scientific classification of the shortfin mako shark goes like this:

- Kingdom: Animalia (all animals)
- Phylum: Chordata (all chordates)
- Class: Chondrichthyes (cartilaginous fish)
- Order: Lamniformes (mackerel sharks)
- Family: Lamnidae (mackerel sharks)
- Genus: Isurus
- Species: oxyrinchus

Every shark belongs to the classification Chondrichthyes which identifies them as cartilaginous fish, fish whose internal skeletons are comprised of flexible cartilage rather than bone.

Chondrichthyes consists of two groups, Holocephali and Elasmobranchii, and within Elasmobranchii are eight (8) orders of sharks. Each order tells us about the biology, physical characteristics and behavior of sharks in that order. Provided here are a number of sharks within each of the eight (8) orders.

Carcharhiniformes

Also known as "ground sharks," carcharhiniformes is largest order of sharks. Their characteristics include five (5) gill slits, moveable eyelids which protect their eyes from injury, two (2) spineless dorsal fins, an anal fin, and a wide mouth filled with sharp teeth located behind the eyes.

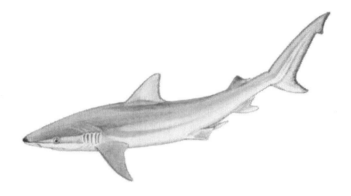

- Blacknose shark - Carcharhinus acronotus

- Blacktip reef shark

- Blacktip Shark

- Blue shark

- Brown Shyshark

- Bull Shark

- Caribbean Reef Shark

- Bronze whaler shark

- Dusky shark

- Galapagos shark

- Great hammerhead shark

- Grey reef shark

- Leopard shark
- Oceanic whitetip shark
- Pacific sharpnose shark
- Pyjama shark
- Sand tiger shark
- Scalloped hammerhead shark
- Sharptooth lemon shark
- Silky shark
- Silvertip shark
- Silvertip shark
- Smooth hammerhead
- Smoothhound
- Spinner shark
- Tiger shark

Heterodontiformes

This is a small order of sharks with only nine (9) known species. They have five (5) gill slits, a dorsal fin with a strong spine and both sharp and flat rounded teeth in their mouth.

Horn shark

Hexanchiformes

Considered the most primitive order of sharks alive today, these sharks have six (6) or seven (7) gill slits, a single dorsal fin, an anal fin and thorny teeth. Most live in cold, deep water.

Bluntnose sixgill shark

Broadnose sevengill shark

Frilled shark

Sharpnose sevengill shark

Lamniformes

These sharks have five (5) gill slits, a large mouth with several rows of sharp teeth, two (2) dorsal fins, an anal fin, and are able to maintain a higher body temperature than the water in which they are swimming.

- Basking shark
- Bigeye thresher shark
- Crocodile shark
- Goblin shark
- Longfin mako shark
- Megamouth shark
- Porbeagle shark
- Salmon shark
- Shortfin mako shark
- White shark

Orectolobiformes

Among the most diverse order of sharks, these sharks have five (5) gill slits, two (2) spineless dorsal fins, an anal fin, and spiracles near their eyes. Most have a patterned skin, and some have barbels on their chins.

- Bluegrey Carpet Shark
- Epaulette shark
- Nurse shark
- Spotted wobbegong
- Tawny nurse shark
- Whale shark
- Whitespotted bamboo shark
- Zebra shark
- Scrapbooking,

Pristiophoriformes

Also known as sawsharks, these sharks have long saw-like snouts. These sharks have five (5) or six (6) gill slits, two (2) dorsal fins, no anal fin, wide pectoral fins and transverse teeth. Most sharks in this order live tropical coastal waters.

Bahamas sawshark

Squaliformes

With an estimated 126 different species, this order of sharks is found in nearly every marine habitat. These sharks have long snouts with a short mouth, five (5) gill slits, two (2) dorsal fins and lack an anal fin.

Some deepwater Squaliformes are bioluminescent.

- Bramble shark

- Cookiecutter shark

- Great Lanternshark

- Greenland shark

- Gulper shark

- Kitefin shark

- Pacific sleeper shark

- Pygmy shark

- Spiny dogfish

Squatiniformes

Sharks in this order have flattened bodies, a mouth with dermal flaps in front of a short snout, nasal barbels, eyes and spiracle on the top of their head, and lack an anal fin.

Angel shark

The 10 Largest Sharks

10. Pacific Sleeper Shark (Somniosus pacificus) 14.4 feet / 4.4m

This shark from the North Pacific feeds on bottom animals. They're known to eat giant octopus. They're fairly productive and their litter sizes are estimated to be around 300. They're often prey to killer whales.

9. Bluntnose Sixgill Shark (Hexanchus griseus) 15.8 feet / 4.8m

This deepwater shark is found around the world in tropical and temperate waters. It spends most of it life in deep water, where it feeds on anything they can find, from crabs to other sharks. Females can give birth to over 100 pups at once.

8. Thresher Shark (Alopias vulpinus) 18.8 feet / 5.73 m

The thresher shark has one of the biggest ranges of all sharks. It's found everywhere except polar waters. About half of its length is due to their enormous tail, which they use to generate great power when they swim.

7. Great Hammerhead Shark (Sphyrna mokarran) 20 feet / 6.1m

The great hammerhead is the largest species of hammerhead. It is found in warm waters around the world. Due to their size they're potentially dangerous to divers, but there are no confirmed attacks on record. Unfortunately their numbers are declining due to the shark fin trade.

6. Great White Shark (Carcharodon carcharias) 20 feet / 6.1 m

The greatest predator on Earth, the great white is famous worldwide for hunting ability. They feed mostly on mammals like seals, dolphins and porpoises, and also fish like sharks and rays. They hold the record for the most bites on humans among all sharks, but most are exploratory bites, where the shark is trying to figure out if they is edible. In most cases, great sharks are more interested in fattier prey such as seals.

5. Greenland Shark (Somniosus microcephalus) 24 feet / 7.3m

The Greenland shark is found in the North Atlantic. It's one of the few filter feeder sharks and eats mostly plankton. It is extremely long-lived, with some individuals thought to be over 300 years old. They reach sexual maturity at around 100 years of age. This shark is completely harmless to divers, but its meat is poisonous.

4. Tiger Shark (Galeocerdo cuvier) 24.6 feet / 7.5 m

Tiger sharks are highly migratory and are found in most of the world's temperate and tropical waters. They're nocturnal opportunistic eaters and will eat anything from turtles to other sharks. They're also very productive, and can have over 80 pups in a litter. Their most salient characteristic is the stripes on their sides. This species has the second most recorded attacks on humans. But despite their ferocity, they're known to be taken by groups of killer whales.

3. Megamouth Shark (Megachasma pelagios) 25 feet / 7.6 meters

This giant is a plankton eater found in all oceans, but it's most commonly spotted in the Pacific. The largest specimen ever found was caught and released in California.

2. Basking Shark (Cetorhinus maximus) 49.8 feet / 15.2 m

A filter feeder, the basking shark is big enough to swallow you whole, but it's completely harmless to humans. They're diet consists of mostly of plankton, which they consume by the pound with their huge mouth, which can open over 1 m wide. These sharks are highly migratory and are known to cover distances of over 9,000 Km a year.

1. Whale Shark (Rhincodon typus) 55.7 feet / 17 m

The largest fish in the world, the whale shark, is an endangered species found in most of the world's tropical waters. Like the megamouth sharks and the basking shark, whale sharks are filter feeders and their diet consists almost exclusively of plankton. Because of this they're completely harmless to humans, and diving with whale sharks has become a popular ecotourism attraction in several countries. While looking for food, whale sharks move their head from side and open and close their gills to get rid of excess of water. The largest individuals can weigh over 30 tonnes and give birth to 300 pups.

Sharks Facts That May Surprise You

1. Sharks do not have bones.

Sharks use their gills to filter oxygen from the water. They are a special type of fish known "elasmobranch", which translates into fish made of cartilaginous tissues—the clear gristly stuff that your ears and nose tip are made of. This category also includes rays, sawfish, and skates. Their cartilaginous skeletons are much lighter than true bone and their large livers are full of low-density oils, both helping them to be buoyant.

Even though sharks don't have bones, they still can fossilize. As most sharks age, they deposit calcium salts in their skeletal cartilage to strengthen it. The dried jaws of a shark appear and feel heavy and solid; much like bone. These same minerals allow most shark skeletal systems to fossilize quite nicely. The teeth have enamel so they show up in the fossil record too.

2. Most sharks have good eyesight.

Most sharks can see well in dark lighted areas, have fantastic night vision, and can see colors. The back of sharks' eyeballs have a reflective layer of tissue called a tapetum. This helps sharks see extremely well with little light.

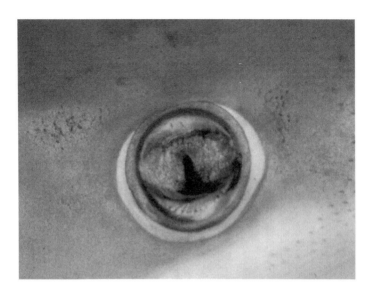

3. Sharks have special electroreceptor organs.

Sharks have small black spots near the nose, eyes, and mouth. These spots are the ampullae of Lorenzini – special electroreceptor organs that allow the shark to sense electromagnetic fields and temperature shifts in the ocean.

4. Shark skin feels similar to sandpaper.

Shark skin feels exactly like sandpaper because it is made up of tiny teeth-like structures called placoid scales, also known as dermal denticles. These scales point towards the tail and help reduce friction from surrounding water when the shark swims.

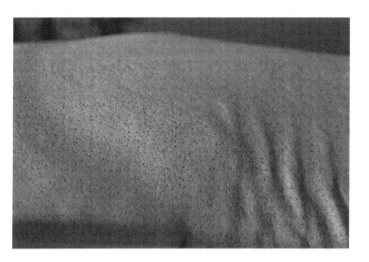

5. Sharks can go into a trance.

When you flip a shark upside down they go into a trance like state called tonic immobility. This is the reason why you often see sawfish flipped over when our scientists are working on them in the water.

6. Sharks have been around a very long time.

Based on fossil scales found in Australia and the United States, scientists hypothesize sharks first appeared in the ocean around 455 million years ago.

7. Scientists age sharks by counting the rings on their vertebrae.

Vertebrae contain concentric pairs of opaque and translucent bands. Band pairs are counted like rings on a tree and then scientists assign an age to the shark based on the count. Thus, if the vertebrae has 10 band pairs, it is assumed to be 10 years old. Recent studies, however, have shown that this assumption is not always correct. Researchers must therefore study each species and size class to determine how often the band pairs are deposited because the deposition rate may change over time. Determining the actual rate that the bands are deposited is called "validation".

8. Blue sharks are really blue.

The blue shark displays a brilliant blue color on the upper portion of its body and is normally snowy white beneath. The mako and porbeagle sharks also exhibit a blue coloration, but it is not nearly as brilliant as that of a blue shark. In life, most sharks are brown, olive, or grayish.

9. Each whale shark's spot pattern is unique as a fingerprint.

Whale sharks are the biggest fish in the ocean. They can grow to 12.2 meters and weigh as much as 40 tons by some estimates! Basking sharks are the world's second largest fish, growing as long as 32 feet and weighing more than five tons.

10. Some species of sharks have a spiracle that allows them to pull water into their respiratory system while at rest. Most sharks have to keep swimming to pump water over their gills.

A shark's spiracle is located just behind the eyes which supplies oxygen directly to the shark's eyes and brain. Bottom dwelling sharks, like angel sharks and nurse sharks, use this extra respiratory organ to breathe while at rest on the seafloor. It is also used for respiration when the shark's mouth is used for eating.

11. Not all sharks have the same teeth.

Mako sharks have very pointed teeth, while white sharks have triangular, serrated teeth. Each leave a unique, tell-tale mark on their prey. A sandbar shark will have around 35,000 teeth over the course of its lifetime!

12. Different shark species reproduce in different ways.

Sharks exhibit a great diversity in their reproductive modes. There are oviparous (egg-laying) species and viviparous (live-bearing) species. Oviparous species lay eggs that develop and hatch outside the mother's body with no parental care after the eggs are laid.

Printed in Great Britain
by Amazon